MY FATHER'S CUP

TOM
WAYMAN

MY FATHER'S CUP

HARBOUR PUBLISHING

Harbour Publishing
P.O. Box 219
Madeira Park, BC
Canada V0N 2H0

THE CANADA COUNCIL | LE CONSEIL DES ARTS
FOR THE ARTS | DU CANADA
SINCE 1957 | DEPUIS 1957

Website: www.harbourpublishing.com

We acknowledge the financial support of the Government of Canada through the Book Publishing Industry Development Program for our publishing activities. We further acknowledge the support of the Canada Council for the Arts and the Province of British Columbia through the British Columbia Arts Council for our publishing program.

Printed in Canada
Cover photograph by Rick Blacklaws

National Library of Canada Cataloguing in Publication Data

Wayman, Tom, 1945–
  My father's cup

Poems.
ISBN 1-55017-282-4

I. Title.
PS8595.A9M92 2002   C811'.54   C2002-910578-1
PR9199.3.W39M92 2002

*In memory of my father and mother
Morris Wayman and Sara Zadkin Wayman*

ACKNOWLEDGEMENTS

My thanks to the editors of the following publications in which poems here appeared or have been accepted for publication:

Arc: Circle
Blade: Boss, The Reef
Denver Quarterly: The Anti-Prometheus
Event: At Dusk, the Deer Move to Water; Epithalamium for a Former
    Lover; On Perry Ridge; Overtaking the Dead; The Pond
The Fiddlehead: On Eby's Path
5 AM: God Hates Hair; The Order in Which We Do Things; Two Poets
    I Admire Contact Me on the Same Day
Hawai'i Review: Negotiations
The Hudson Review: Apparition
The Iowa Review: The Blossoming; Kosovo
The Malahat Review: Hawk; Photon; What a Word Lacks
The Massachusetts Review: Cup; It's Friday
Mercury: Nineteen Ninety-nine
The New Quarterly: Big Weather; A Meeting With Neruda in Toronto
North Dakota Quarterly: Excursion
Ontario Review: Ice Lake; Moving to Heaven; The Quiet of the Seven
    Sisters; The Road Father
Queen's Quarterly: Soaring Crow
Willow Springs: Fear Eclipsed by Distance; For Bill Sutherland;
    Gesture; The Nap; A Smaller Table
Windsor Review: Absence

I very much appreciate support from The Canada Council and the BC
Arts Council, which assisted in the writing and assembly of this book.

CONTENTS

A SMALLER TABLE

HAWK

North of Paso Robles, a hawk
is buoyed far over a sloped vineyard
by the wind pushing hard along the river
south from Monterey Bay.
Oak and eucalyptus groves
stagger under the fierce gusts
the predator above kites insouciantly on.

My father is dying. Below his hospital window
three hundred miles from this valley
an expanse of parked vehicles is visible
and beyond them a line of palms. At my back, my father
lies dazed, or asleep. In the flawless blue
a hawk lifts and wheels.

                Perhaps my father is not dying
but only very sick. His body withered,
mouth fallen backwards into his face,
tubes connect him to the walls of this building;
he is diapered and catheterized.
When I bend above him
he says he is finished, that he wants
this life to be over, he would ask my help
with assisted suicide—except, he assures me, he is aware
the act is illegal. He speaks the same words
to his doctors,
and, his voice urgent, groans
or shouts with pain when he is turned or hoisted erect.
Each quarter-hour a bodily function
is measured by a sharpened apparatus
whose insertion through his skin generates
an additional tiny agony. His legs hurt, his bedsores.

      The hawk here tugs at the invisible string
      holding it to earth, as it banks

at the furthest reach of its tether,
coasts upwind toward
King City and Soledad.

My father's speech begins to blur, then clear,
then fog again; sometimes he is not certain
of the time of day, day of the week.
After eighty years of attentive reading
his eyes reject even a newspaper.
Blood appears in his catheter bag—the dark fluid
discounted by one doctor, worrisome to another.

A television in the room
watched by an old man in the other bed,
gibbers and hums incessantly, the sound
applauded by sets audible from every doorway
along this ward, as each device
stridently promotes its objects or services
to the aged and very ill.

The hawk ascends in the rising wind. The hawk.
The short-lived hawk.

EXCURSION

I watched him sleep for hours
one afternoon, propped on his side by the nurses.
His stick limbs twitched uncomfortably every few moments
into slight shifts in position
—all he could manage in his weakness—
as his fingers frequently plucked air
in the manner my mother, his wife, did for weeks
as she slept toward death.

A cacophony of television pounded at me:
from the machine watched by the old man
on the further side of the curtain,
so only inches from my ear,
and from across the hall
and more rooms down the corridor.
At last I stood, and requested the figure in the other bed
to turn his volume down
which he did, and the noises that continued
gradually receded in my mind
as I sat where my father dreamed.

When he woke
he asked me to remain through his supper.
And after he had pushed away his tray,
the meal not half-eaten,
he wanted to sit in his wheelchair.

I found the nurse
and helped where I could as she carefully
heaved and coaxed his painful limbs
first upright, then across the frightful gap
between mattress and seat
and then to a more comfortable arrangement.
Once he collected himself, he suggested I push him
down the ward.

The request surprised me.
He had been clinging to despair, indifferent
to a cheerful prognosis, emphatic that he was terminal,
that to be through with his life
was his foremost wish. He was impatient with me now,
as often in his sickness, when I questioned
a voyage out of the room
—so unlike his usual behavior these days—
and again when I inquired would he be warm enough?
Should I fetch his sweater?

                The chair
had no foot rests, and his bluish feet
hurt him. He was wary of my clumsiness
and shouted orders and cautions as we began.
But for the first time in days
he was mobile: through the room's furniture to the hall
and down it to the main entrance
where he asked to go outside.

                      I struggled with his conveyance
through the double doors
into the subtropical evening.
On a stoop
at the top of stairs leading to a parking area
with a treed boulevard beyond,
I set the brakes and he sat
and gazed at the fan palms
and bougainvillea, heard the chittering of small birds
transporting themselves from eucalpytus to oleander,
the faint pulses of distant traffic.

I inspected his face,
shrunken to an unfamiliar mouth
now sagged permanently
into disapproval.
As long as I had known him

he delighted in sunsets
and people's gardens along a sidewalk,
would pause to admire hummingbirds
or crows, treescapes and a single tall birch
branchless nearly to the crown.
On his wheelchair in the warm dusk
he did not speak.
I tried to read his eyes: were they reconsidering
his determination to leave this world?
Or staring a farewell?
We can go in whenever you like
he said, startling the silence.
I maneuvered him back between the doors
through the clamor and humming of the televisions
to his bed.

      That night
his sheets filled with blood,
the onset of the flow
no one could
staunch.

CUP

Because of heavy painkillers
administered to my father
or a deep dream,
before he died he called out from a doze in his wheelchair:
Take, take it.
His tone was desperate, so I stepped closer
to reassure: *It's all right. You were asleep.*
What's the matter?
His eyes now gaped at his world:
the curtain isolating him from the other bed here,
a portable commode, his wheeled tray
holding an untouched lunch of broth and jello.
Then he recognized me and said:
I was drinking a cup of coffee
with nowhere to put it down.
His voice was anxious and bewildered so I soothed:
It was just a dream; don't worry.
But he said: *Take it from me,*
anyway. After a moment
I reached across his lap to seize
a cup of nothing
which I held to my chest as I straightened again.
My father smiled slightly
at the oddity of this event
and slept. Thus his cup
passed to me.

KOSOVO

My father died in Kosovo.
The terrifying screech of a jet passing low overhead
is gigantic, but if such an aircraft
releases cannon fire into streets and buildings
or sticks of bombs stream from other planes far above,
even more frightening
is the unrelenting concussive roar
while houses and bridges and pavement
erupt, then crumble into metal shards and
mounds of splintered limbs. All this rage
directed at you
ignores your desire to keep breathing.
How hard to be eighty-four and frail and dying
when the young are determined to murder you.

My father died in Kosovo.
The hospital he was in remained operational
with full electric power
and a competent staff to tend him
where he lay intubated
by a tangle of IVs, catheter, leads to monitors,
and with pain searing down his legs,
the skin of his lower back
open in a raw sore, fecal material
lodged in and ulcerating his rectum
so his diaper was filled with blood
each time it was changed.
And the tonnage of high explosives expended
doubled and tripled until

my father died in Kosovo. The televisions
throughout the hospital explained many times
how regrettable but necessary this war was.
My father did not pay attention.
His hearing aid had been lost during a transfer

to ICU one night, or to an operating room for a colonoscopy
one afternoon, so he couldn't hear
what the announcers uttered.
Also, this was the tenth or maybe eleventh war
in his lifetime so far
during which electrical apparatuses had pronounced
the same words. He had lost count,

yet he died in Kosovo.
The hospital wanted to keep old men like my father
alive, doctors kept puzzling in groups over his symptoms
out by the nursing station,
referring to charts and CAT scans,
pumping drugs into him, insisting
his body be turned and fed and that
someone shave and sponge him.
But on every side soldiers
were ordered to operate devices designed
to blow open human bodies of every age,
to crush and sever
heads, torsos, organs of the elderly.

My father told his doctors he wanted to die.
He repeatedly said he no longer wanted to live. One physician
decided my father must be crazy. Why would anyone
not want to live
while Kosovo was under siege, before somebody could learn
the way this conflict would end?
This man commanded my father be transferred
to a psychiatric institution
also still untouched by shells or mortar attack.
My father never understood the reason
he was moved there: the place was intended
to have its inmates sit each day
on worn sofas and talk about their problems. My father
could not change position in bed without assistance
and spasms of convulsive pain.
How can a person become so weak

he is unable to roll himself over?
My father was that feeble: to maneuver him erect,
then off the mattress onto a wheelchair,
into which he had to be strapped,
also took great effort and dexterity
on the part of a nurse or nurse's aide,
accompanied by protests and yells of anguish
from my father. Though the psychiatric facility
was not equipped to offer such services, days were required
to return my father to a hospital

and each transfer meant more suffering:
the gurney hard as a plank to lie on,
so my father shook with agony, gripping the rails
and calling for relief
from the piercing flames melting the flesh of his back.
There was no relief. My father refused food,

they transferred him to a hospice ward,
and he died in Kosovo
as the missiles descended, people were burned alive
in cities and villages
and out on the roads; nearly all the men shot
older than a certain age
were fathers. They were not my father.
My father died in Kosovo.

GESTURE

Through a doorway I hear the gabble of
the living room filled with people
—mainly elderly, most of whom I've never met before—
who have gathered for a little afternoon party
to display respect for my father's death
a few days previously. The guests,
residents of this retirement village
to which my father moved three years ago,
salute each other and gossip
as they drift to the table where the cakes and pastries
and vegetable dips are arranged; each attendee
grips a paper napkin, small paper plate
and plastic cup of punch or juice.
From the swarm of bodies surrounding the food
they emerge to reform into threesomes or one-on-ones
—either standing, or according to whether
space is left on a sofa
or how easily smaller chairs can be repositioned.
A few shuffle out to the patio
to gaze for a moment across the lawn
at the magnificent roses my father loved,
with their attendant bougainvillea, peaches, lemons.

I have been sent
to the kitchen to make coffee. The guests,
having now discharged their funereal obligation
—leavened somewhat by chattering with acquaintances
they haven't spoken to since yesterday
or the weekend,
are starting to indicate impending departure.
The percolator I have been assigned
is new to me, but I am cognizant
of its operating principle: fill the pot with water
to a volume shown by marks
on the pot's insides, add a corresponding amount

of ground coffee to the holed basket,
cap basket and pot, plug in.

                I cast my eye along the counter
to locate the cannister of coffee.
Nearby, though, I recognize the container that holds
my father's ashes
deposited in someone's fluster
after a helpful guest stopped at the funeral home en route
and delivered the urn here together with some requested
extra avocados and soda.

              I don't even hesitate.
I pry the lid off the urn
and carefully measure out sixteen spoonfuls
for the percolator's basket. I snap everything
into its proper place, then step back
as the heated water begins to cheerfully gargle and clatter.
Is it brewed yet? a voice inquires from the doorway.
Just about, I reply, pleased at this opportunity to offer
the only suitable beverage for such an occasion,
the right concoction
to observe disappearing down the throats
of all the assholes still alive.

A SMALLER TABLE

My mother in a good dress, with her hair well coifed,
is bent forward at the sideboard to examine
the jammed cluster of sympathy cards
received after her death, and, more recently,
my father's
He is present as well, though her intense absorption with
the array of cards
matches how I remember her repeated inventory of
Christmas greetings
displayed on a shelf or fireplace mantel
—since sometimes one of my parents, sometimes the other
opened their mail

Behind the pair is a dining room table
at which my mother and father, my brother, and I
have eaten
Yet it is time for the next meal
The plates, cloth serviettes, cutlery, glasses
are set for only two, on a tabletop
not much larger than necessary to hold these objects
and lower by six inches than the kitchen counter
the smaller table abuts
My father speaks, his voice twisted
by an anguish I cannot bear: "Look what our family
has shrunk to."
I put my arms around his sorrow to comfort him
and find myself weeping for the first time
since my parents died: "You can come with
me, Dad. I want you to stay with me."
But my father shakes his head
"I can't
live with you," he decrees wearily
and I immediately comprehend
why his decision is irrefutable
The woody note of a clarinet or oboe

swells from nothing to
a round fullness, tasting of butter, of cloves
Then air starts to splinter around it, the sound
gutters away to silence
My brother and I sit facing each other
across our empty plates
to eat what is put in front of us

THE NAP

My mother shrivelled on the big double bed, very sick now,
and my brother helped tend her.

                        One evening a month before
my mother struggled shakily from the dim bedroom
and announced to my brother and father and me
still seated at the dining table: *I fear*
I am slipping away.

           We tried to drown
this message: insisted this could not be so,
the medication for her stomach probably was affecting her,
assured her she would feel better
with a good night's sleep

                 but in that sleep
no doctor afterwards could tell us
what occurred

              —except she could no longer talk
though she strained and stretched her mouth
around the vowels, consonants, striving to utter
words as we bent
close to her lips, asking asking
Are you hungry? Too cold? Is the light
bothering you? while an angry
dismissive impatience
flared across her face
and sounds gurgled and
stuttered from her

            until she lost energy
and subsided. Nor could she anymore
write
or read

so she had no words at all.

Then she wanted no bedclothes, either,
or any clothes: tugging off even her diaper
and lying naked, trying from time to time to claw
the IV from her skin.

                      Yet other than such vexed moments,
her eyes became anxious to please
like those of a little girl
desperate to be good.
They shone
when one homecare nurse she evidently liked
came on shift. And my anguished father
now spoke steadily to her
as one talks lovingly to the very young: the first instances
in my life
I heard him pronounce endearments to her
though whether she comprehended
who these people trying to help her were
was unclear, but her eyes begged
Be kind to me;
oh, thank you
for your kindness

                or were fierce with
pain that she cried aloud
when she had to be turned for bathing, or
to change the underlay pad, or sheets.

                        And my brother
cheerfully figured how best
to provide water on a sponge, to spoon in applesauce,
arrange her pillows most comfortably:
once you've raised kids,
he said, *you can handle these situations*
—even the horror of
a subcutaneous saline drip gone wrong

so one of her breasts swelled with fluid
which began to leak from the nipple
until the error was noticed
and a jostling flurry of those around her
solved that crisis.

And once, on an afternoon
while my mother dozed, my brother,
who had been up at dawn to prepare for work
and had stopped in at noon for an hour
and as the winter day slowed to a close
was back, stretched himself next to her
to rest for a minute, rather than nod
in a chair. My mother's eyes
opened wide
when the mattress took his weight.
She stared at him,
then seemed to recognize who he was
and her face smiled and
her eyelids lowered again. She slept
and beside her my brother slept
—mother by son,
child by parent—
until the darkness woke them.

APPARITION

From my kitchen window I see
the shoulders of my dead mother
hunched forward to work at a bush of my red roses,
a bed of gladioli,
with that persistence of hers I recall:
weed, trim the dead blooms,
rake fertilizer into the soil.
She wears her red cardigan
with silvered buttons—a garment
she bought in Finland, now darned many places,
her choice for gardening in coolish weather.

What brings her this August afternoon
to my lawns and perennials?
This summer I meant to create
a memorial planting for her between my house
and the woods—developed a design,
bought four-by-four beams
to build a retaining structure, had a small plaque made.
But the weeks passed in setting out annuals,
in hours behind the mower, and crouched over to tend
and thin my new lettuce and carrots and corn.
Each green stem—wanted or not—obstinately insists
on its right to rise, to flourish.
So my project in her honor was delayed.

Perhaps as in life her object is
to assist me:
not as a reproach to my tardiness
but a contribution to my chores.

Alive, she was this fiercely stubborn
in support of my ventures
—albeit cautiously questioning,
to be certain in her own mind

my plans would be good for me. Yet she was unfailing
in her endorsement
of whatever I attempted.

And, as now,
she would contribute if she could,
dogged in her determination to aid,
dogged as chickweed,
as the roses thriving where her shoulder was.

ABSENCE

I do not want my parents to be lost.
My mother grew a fear as she aged
that my father would suddenly vanish: I remember her fury
when in the country my father
one afternoon took some vegetables over to a neighbor
and my mother later shouted at him
that for an hour she did not know
if he was face down amidst the tall corn
with a heart attack, or struck by a car on the road.
Yet it was she who wandered to where
she could not be reached
and left him with his basket of pea-pods and beans,
the squash still swelling on the vines.
In her sickness, small stroke after stroke
dissolved her personality, simplified it,
then precipitated it out as a child without speech
who nevertheless felt pain and discomfort
and a wondering delight whenever she encountered
some person or act that pleased her.

If my parents had to be lost,
I wished for them to go missing together
like the elderly couple found dead
in their overturned car down an embankment
of a mountain highway.

                        But my father lived on by himself
when there was no more news of my mother,
heating his lonely can of soup at noon.
He blundered past the sympathy of his friends,
compiling a catalogue of petty slights.
He blurted amorous suggestions
painful to near-strangers and to women
he had known for forty years

and flared with angry dismissals of
people, ideas, plans.

                    He emerged from time to time
from this haze of enforced solitude
but the mist reformed around him
until there were only
rows of lettuce and carrots and onions
drowsing in the heat.

                    I try to imagine him and my mother
walking once more side by side
through a wooded place
down a track not made by tool or shoe or hoof.
But I sense my mother and father voyage alone,
poised to unload their grievances on each other
should they meet
with a fierce relief. A fog of blood and air
separates them
and them from me.
I want my parents not to be lost.

BEQUEST

Last day of August; the previous night
cool and wet, so before the sun tops the east ridge
fog lies heavy over the river.
This morning for the first time
the light in the birch and aspen leaves
is autumn's—paler, more diffuse.
On the summits that surround the valley
are swathes of fresh white, with the tallest peaks
blurred by cold mists
of blowing snow.

                That clouded region
at the edges of the sky
is where I must travel. My parents
have disappeared.
My task is to retrace their passage, to
discover what they have become.

I steer my truck up a forestry road,
a single lane that twists between cutbanks
amid stands of cedar
where the creeks flow down, then spruce,
and clusters of larch whose needles
have not yet turned. The route
has been bulldozed through mounds of till
and debris flow; run-off has gouged small gullies
and stripped soil from boulders
underlying the right-of-way. Here and there
somebody has dumped gravel to restore
the surface. In spots,
one shoulder of the road falls sharply into a wooded canyon;
other places, my vehicle travels through a hollow,
slopes lifting on both sides.

              As the track climbs

the air harshens and thins. A chill
sears my nose and throat
through my open window. Purple fireweed,
the intense red of Indian paintbrush
and even a few blue lupine raise points of color
on disturbed ground near the road.
But the pines have become smaller and sparser
among open spaces
where the tough grasses
bend in the wind. Pools of snow
appear under the branches
and then the route degrades to
parallel ruts separated by
an intermittent band of low weeds and bushes.
Not long after, a dusting
lies across the road.

Tire treads precede me through the white,
though whether the other vehicle
has returned or is still above me
I cannot determine. At last
on a flat stretch where the route widens slightly
a display of churned and trampled snow
reveals where someone carefully manoeuvred
to swing around. I push forward
along an undisturbed track.

                          Cloud or fog
drifts through the trees ahead
and then I am within the wet whiteness.
I roll my window up
and activate the truck's wipers and defrost.
Snow is packed heavier on the earth
as I ease cautiously across
the uneven mounds of a small excavation
below a cliff-face. Past this, I am uncertain
where the road leads.

I shut the engine off,
sit for a minute in the deep quiet.
When I open the door, I hear
a rising of the alpine wind.
I remove my key from the ignition
and step out into snow
that reaches the ankles of my boots.
I place the truck key on the seat
and close the door. After decades of care,
of vigilance, what I own
I no longer need,
is no more mine.
I zipper my jacket
and start to trudge upslope.

                                             I watch my breath ascend
as I heave myself onward. Snow clings
to the limbs of fir I climb among.
Wisps of cloud hover in their branches
and overhead up the draw.
My eyes dart about for any sign
of my mother and father, of their
presence here.

                         A tree has blown down across my path
and I bend to struggle under the trunk
through the tangle of snowy limbs. I straighten
on the further side, and scan a steep rise:
a jumble of deadfall below the standing timber
and no way up evident. I glance around,
stalled amid the resigned soughing
of the icy air, and feel my parents' hands
at my back, pressing me
to find them, be where they are.
With each step, my boots lose traction, slipping
on frozen bark or rock, or bursting through crust
onto clumps of dormant bearberry or juniper.
When I pause

to try to breathe normally again,
cold settles on my skin like a shroud.

THE POND

THE QUIET OF THE SEVEN SISTERS

I remember the quiet of the Seven Sisters
you said, meaning the grove of the tallest trees
on my acreage: five firs

an alder, a pine
soaring sixty feet or more
as we lay on our backs

under them on a Mexican blanket
holding hands, naked as the summer
after making love

I recall watching the afternoon sun
pass in the leaves, and a slight breeze
and the cries of robin and thrush

and not one thing that hot day cared
that I stood alone and frightened
on a pier

while an ocean liner, painted entirely black
as if in camouflage from some war
carried you away

EPITHALAMIUM FOR A FORMER LOVER

Let her rose stems droop,
And the blooms be leprous and dulled.

Let the place of ceremony have
Off-green cement block walls, unrelieved by ornament,

And be lit by one fluorescent fixture
Whose sole functioning tube flickers and hums.

May the closest parking lot
Be three blocks away

And the wedding party drenched by a sudden hailstorm
As they scurry toward the building.

May an old girlfriend of the groom's
Appear uninvited,

Obviously stoned, who talks loudly and incomprehensibly
To those seated on either side of her

Even once the ritual starts.
Let the presiding official

Be so elderly he must be assisted to the front
Dressed inappropriately in a stained sweatsuit

And during a rambling preliminary discourse
Refer to the nuptial couple

By the wrong names several times
In the course of arguments intended to prove

The area has been repeatedly visited by alien spacecraft.
Even when a member of the audience

Manages to blurt out a gentle correction
Concerning the name of the bride and groom,

The official, once he finally comprehends the issue,
Commits the same error seconds later.

Let the ex-girlfriend's commentary on the incident
So provoke the groom's Uncle Reggie, already largely drunk,

That he opines she should shut her face.
May her reply, involving unique and imaginative profanity,

Inspire Reggie to leap from his seat
And attempt to resolve their divergent views

On acceptable wedding decorum
By physical means.

Let chairs around the dispute
Be tipped over as shoving and pushing commence

And someone yells out the police have been notified.
May the police take nearly an hour to respond to the call

During which a cluster of the younger guests
Forms around the antagonists in an attempt to restrain them,

While the rest of the assembly
Forms small groups engaged in spirited debate

Over the merits of the semifinal contenders of some sport,
Or whether Alex has a chance with Lucia

On *Days of Our Lives*.
Let moments before the arrival of a patrolman

The presiding official announce he is late for a different appointment
And shuffle out of the hall

Considerately leaving his paperwork behind.
So when the constable shows up

He must be importuned into completing the ceremony
Which, after handcuffing the ex-girlfriend,

Loading her into the rear of his cruiser,
And ordering Uncle Reggie off the premises,

He does. Then as everyone crowds around the now-united pair,
Let the cell phone of the bride's brother

Inform the gathering
The house where the reception is to be held

Has just been burglarized, with most of the wedding gifts
Stolen, along with a packet of congratulatory communications

Temporarily stored in a
Silver-plated gravy tureen,

Including a postcard I sent—with six cents postage due—
That wishes the two, however briefly their marriage might last,

All the joy they deserve.

PHOTON

> "Something traveling at light speed through space
> will have no speed left for motion through time.
> Thus light does not get old; a photon that emerged
> from the big bang is the same age today it was
> then."
> —Brian Greene, *The Elegant Universe*

If the physicists are right, we are surrounded by
much that does not age:
infrared, X-ray, microwaves
and visible light,
which are also convertible to mass
—filling this universe
with the immortal. In our own brief flourishing,
our eyes continually encounter
what time cannot debase,
sicken, end.

Thus we do not have to look far
to elude the temporal.
No wonder incarnations of the divine
or the unearthly wise
appear wrapped in a nimbus or halo
composed of an unchanging truth

and that the urge to forward through time
who we are, the impulse
to preserve everything possible of ourselves
for the future,
is enacted via an electromagnetic event:
our bodies sag, but the orgasm, too,
never grows old.
Neurons firing simultaneously
throughout the brain

exchange with each other
the immutable cosmic substance.
For that instant, we hold
eternities of pleasure
in a single cell.
We touch within our minds
what light must feel at maximum velocity, the
ecstasy of reaching
every place at once, of ceaseless be-
coming.

THE POND

My kisses across her skin
    in the dimmed light—
a latticework of motion: breezes
    in the columbine, or a filigree
of aspen leaves rustling through July heat

    My lips on her arms, stomach, thighs
release concentric rings
    flowing outward over her flesh
—as by a pond shaded by hazel and balsam
    small creatures lower their heads to lap water

then lift tiny muzzles
    to emit exuberant cries
at the ecstasy in their throats, their mouths
    thick with such satisfaction, such desire

THE ORDER IN WHICH WE DO THINGS

TREASON OF THE CLERKS

Nine a.m. at the corner of
Vernon and Ward Streets
of this small city:
for a block or more in each direction
store owners or their employees
are unlocking front doors,
moving the necessary signage or outside displays
onto the sidewalk, putting the cash float
in the registers.

          Past them, along the asphalt,
a loaded logging truck active since before dawn
hauls its third load of the day
to Kalesnikoff's mill.
A welding supply wholesale truck
pulls in from the valley
four hours west. And a power company service van
starts the morning's list of calls
as, one by one, the vehicles of construction contractors
drive out to renovation projects and repairs.

Amid this activity, I stride up Ward,
a file folder beneath my arm.
I am already a few minutes late for a meeting.
On the sidewalk around me materialize
a dozen other men and women
also carrying paper
—in briefcases, envelopes, binders
or clutched in a hand.
They, too, step purposefully toward appointments.
All morning we and others like us
will transport sheaves of paper from desk to counter top,
office to jobsite, conference room
to restaurant. At one locale
we will exchange pages. At a different destination

I will add more sheets to what I bear.
During a gathering with other people,
we will scribble notes on the papers we brought with us
or on blank pads whose contents
later will be transformed into additional pages.
Throughout the afternoon, also,
we will haul paper from block to block,
to deposit and retrieve the piles of
white squares covered with words.

Our comings and goings resemble the weather
in which the tasks of the world
occur: a backdrop, nuisance,
but rarely essential—except where we prevent or delay
what someone needs or desires to achieve.
We are the rainstorm everybody labors through:
either dressed against it, if outside,
or, when employed indoors,
glancing at the windows occasionally
while the storm drums down and then passes.
Except, unlike water, we inexorably emerge
every place work is
the way a haze or smoke appears
each time a certain machine is switched on.

BOSS

Some minds settled in an office
contain a shark
ceaselessly weaving circles
within a skull's glass-sided aquarium
whose walls dissolve at will
and the shark, released, lunges,
tail thrashing water to foam,
to strike a person deemed inferior,
worry the wound, then veer back,
the glass reforming so any onlooker can once more view
the finned menace rotating
in its lair.

   The shark is indiscriminate
about the recipient of this fury: a child-like
or other unprotected being
or fully functional adult.
Always the animal's maximum cunning and strength
—angle of attack, slash of teeth—
is expended, no matter what target.
The provocation
for such assaults is declared later:
some flicker of movement perceived as threatening,
a suggestion of action or behavior
intolerable to a shark.

    If hooked and dragged into air
the beast twists and straightens frantically,
yanking against the rope,
while vocalizing squeaks astonishingly subdued
for the terror its body can create.

     Once beached
the shark in sunlight metamorphoses
into a glistening jellied medusa

that quivers slightly in the salt wind.
Stranded on sand or rock, the creature's fragility
is evident: an air sack from which long tendrils
lie uselessly tangled.
For a time, the thin tentacles possess a sting
if handled incautiously. But the chemical sharpness
the invertebrate can exude
fades quickly,
leaving it defenseless, slumped on dry pebbles
or half-immersed in a tidal pool,
almost inert.

THE REEF

"You mean to say, in your class, we have to read a
whole *book*?"

—first-year college student

As a young person's curiosity
encounters their world,
each chance to absorb,
consider, grow
is a polyp
without tooth or shell.

When such an invertebrate
is injured, it secretes
an external calcareous skeleton. In some cases,
despite this adaptation,
further insult kills the polyp.
But inhabited or not, the jagged skeletons
can accumulate
into a mound, a fence, or over enough time,
a wall.

When I teach someone
thus encumbered,
I try to soften, dissolve
the construction
or bypass it: float above,
tunnel under.

Yet I also want the afflicted
to dismantle the barricade,
to push
a way through, or

cut an opening for a window.

Yet often they cannot circumvent
the rampart
any better than I. *Besides,*
they say,
people like you
put it there. You
figure how to alter it.

Our mutual bafflement
angers us. We glare across the crenelated top
toward one another.
I cannot see in
nor they out.
We speculate: *How stupid*
the person is
on the other side of this obstruction.

Furious, I charge against it,
rebound, my hands and face
scraped, blood oozing. Or they
do.

    Both of us marked
by the stolid viciousness
of this third thing,
we turn,
go to a different place
with someone else.

MAY DAY 2001: NEGOTIATING A NEW COLLECTIVE AGREEMENT

We slide a sheet of green paper
across the table. The three people who face us
regard the page with distaste
or fear or contempt. In their eyes
a small animal—gopher, squirrel—
frantically tests the confines of a trap,
claws clinging to walls, ceiling, walls once more.
The creature calms as our spokesman
begins to explain what we mean the words on the paper
to say.

    We have a response
to one of your earlier proposals
their chief negotiator announces.
Her fingers propel a blue sheet of paper
toward our side. I begin to tense.

How many men and women suffered
for years in how many places
to bring us to this hotel meeting room
with its stiff-backed chairs
to undertake this rite. In our small enterprise, however,
the representatives of the employer opposite me
are not strangers: I spoke earlier with one
about the problems he is having
with the catalytic converter on his pickup,
am acquainted with the person another is dating
after her divorce, am aware two are from union backgrounds
themselves—uneasy in their present role
yet resolute in defending the viewpoint
they feel this room's seating arrangements
entitles them to.

    Our side's troubles
originated not only with our adversaries here

but also when a tribe or settlement
began to fracture, and a certain man
could no longer count on his relatives
or clan to help him locate
a particular errant goat, or to gather
firewood for his sick mother.
In the midst of wanting to denounce again
the contemporary decay of values—as he and two friends
had done last evening around the fire—the man, Ug,
was struck by an idea.
Suppressing his excitement,
Ug strode across the village
to find a neighbor, Og,
and introduce his concept: *Hey, buddy,*
even though you married into our bunch
you seem sort of an outsider around here.
I couldn't help noticing, too,
things have been a little hand-to-mouth for you lately.
How about I pay you
to complete a little task for me.
The brows of the other man furrowed. "Pay?"
Yeah. I'll give you some boar meat I've got smoked
if you'll help me remove stones from that strip of land
between my hut and the river for plowing.
I'd do it myself, but I have this sore arm.

Og's face brightened. "Wow, Ug,
that's truly generous of you.
I could use a patch of ground of my own
to get a few seeds in.
And the wife and kids will really appreciate
the meat. Like you say,
it's been tough couple of months.
What a thoughtful gift
and completely unexpected. You're not even related
to my wife—or are you?"

No, buddy, you don't understand. I'm not about to give

you anything. You do what I ask you over at the field.
In return you acquire
a haunch of smoked boar. Period.

"You mean, like a trade? You want me to trade myself
as if . . . as if I were a spear? Or a pot?"

I never thought of it that way, but, yeah.

"You must be out of your mind, Ug. I'm not some object
I can barter with. I may be low on luck
but I remain a human.
How could you even imagine I'd . . . ?"

But we know how this argument
was resolved, how Ug and Og's eventual arrangement
became the saddest story ever told:
the construct that eons later has brought
our anxious, bristly group to sit around a table
this early Spring morning, on a day that for most of a century
celebrated the dream of the end
of this distribution of privileges and powers.
In 1905 the Wobblies said
one class, one enemy, one union,,
and that *a contract is only a negotiated truce*
in an ongoing war. All of which I believe
but I also see one species
blundering ahead through the ages,
ever uncertain if each individual
alone should take care of himself or herself,
or if a family or town, nation
or occupational group should help bear this responsibility,
or whether none of our separate lives can tangibly improve
apart from all the lives around us
—that being the effect of sharing
a location and clump of years with so many other souls.
In any case, this day intended to honor
the possibility of an entirely different deal

than the current one
flourished and faded in a momentary blip
compared to our tenure as humans.
Yet if we gaze back far enough,
we have managed to dispose of—more or less—
the divine rule of kings, slavery
or equally horrific methods of classifying other people as
inferior, plus laws forbidding
unions or strikes or even increases in wages.
During just the brief period when this festival
was one we proclaimed, enjoyed, and lost again
we can point to the organization of the I.W.W.,
the Ukrainian Makhnovshchina,
the rural communes of Aragon and
the structuring at Barcelona of practical democracy
into industrial ventures

                    —even if
the cluster of employees that includes me
spend today pushing in the direction of some solemn faces
additional provisions on work apportionment,
seniority, and parental leave.
Hours pass in tense forays and retreats
at the table, nervous jokes and shouts of anger
in our breakout room. Our sentences, their sentences
scratch and claw at one another,
as the means we need to exist
or to exist well
are balanced against the thrill of control,
of shaping the world others must inhabit.
Phrases batter phrases,
waves hammering a shoreline
until a section of sandy earth and seagrass
collapses and is swept away,
or rock stands firm,
turning aside what engulfs it
in a spray of words we'll have to live by.
Still to come is new language
on management rights.

NEGOTIATIONS

This landscape is a forest
without undergrowth. Straight trunks
like irregularly placed columns
hold aloft a leafy roof
that darkens the roads and houses
situated under the canopy:
the light here dim sepia in every direction.

A ravine angles through the below-world.
The banks of the gully support an occasional huge tree
that has survived periodic land slips.
A creek at the bottom pushes between low mounds
of earth, rocks, logs, and patches of coarse grass.

At the top of this rift, on either side
an encampment has formed: cookfires flash
through the thick light, smoke wavers upward
toward the covering of the world.
One settlement is large: tents haphazardly placed,
kids racing around, men and women
seated in irregular circles, or standing
talking, or shifting from cluster to cluster,
or tending to small herds
of pack or dairy animals, amid hammer blows
from a blacksmith's portable forge,
and carpenters constructing some sort of booth.
A potter's wheel spins; the wooden framework of a moving loom
patterned with a shiny metal
shoots erratic jets of muted color over
several half-unpacked crates nearby.

Across the divide, the camp is almost silent.
Here tents are fewer, neatly arranged in lines.
The steel points of pikes and swords

racked beside the dwellings glitter.
Streams of sparks flow from a grinding wheel
where two men sharpen blades of axes and knives.
Only a handful of other people are visible;
a tense sullenness hangs over the bivouac.

From each lip of the ravine, half a dozen people
have slid down to the creek
to sit on stones they rolled to one place
where the V of the gully widens a little.
For hours they argue across the water.
The voices floating up from this meeting
sometimes lift into shouts
or edgy laughter
but listeners at the top of the slopes
mostly hear a steady drone.

At intervals, messengers scramble up the bank
toward the more populous group—
their arrival above is greeted
with excitement: a throng of talkers
quickly forms, much information is exchanged
with gestures and some scribbling of words on paper
passed around the assembly
which initiates another round of energetic chatter.
Then the messenger slides and stumbles back down
and the debate at the bottom resumes.
Or, less frequently,
a representative climbs the gully's other side
to be greeted ceremoniously by a sentry
and led to the door of a tent
to which the newcomer is admitted.
Eventually he emerges, salutes the canvas,
and clambers down again to rejoin his party.

After a number of hours, everyone at the bottom of the opening
picks their way up
to rest, or consult further with their own people.

Days, weeks pass in this manner.
In each polity, food and fuel is obtained
and consumed; in one camp
children are born and schooled,
expeditions of traders assemble and depart
and reappear, the sick and elderly
are cared for. When the settlements remain
for more than one season, gardens are cleared
and planted, fencing for horses and cattle
is erected, and if
much yelling and curses have ascended lately
out of the ravine
stockades and other earthworks are constructed
and improved.

One afternoon, though, a traveller
through this part of the woods
finds no trace of either settlement
—the structures dismantled, the earth swept level,
the inhabitants vanished. Every word exchanged here
and whatever was concluded
have been absorbed into the forest.
The cleft in the earth still gapes,
with well-braided trails discernible on the sides of the gully.
Already, however, the edges of these routes down to water
have begun to loose small showers of soil.

IT'S FRIDAY

—payday—and as I scan my stock listings
I want to say to some of you:
thanks, guys
and gals, for your work this week
which through the graces of whoever set certain wheels in motion
has put a sum of your money
in my account, too.
I remember well when I was employed in production
how every Friday the boss pried a swack of dough
right out of my cheque
as soon as the various levels of government
and the company seized their portions. And then I donated
—not that anybody asked if I'd care to indulge
in such beneficence—a heap of change
to a whole gaggle of people
who never punched in here, never had to put up with
Casper, who is always borrowing other people's tools,
leaving them someplace
and then muttering *Oh, yeah* when you ask for them back.
My work made the folks never seen at the assembly station
or up on the scaffold
money
and not one of them ever uttered a word of gratitude.
Now I'm a shareholder myself, I'm saying *Thank you*
—although if you're like me
you'd just as soon have the cash.

Not that I don't work at the moment, either. It's just that
these days every cent I earn comes from taxes
—since I'm in what is jokingly called the service professions,
the education sector, to be precise.
So, hey, I should thank you again
for your willingness—maybe that's not the right word—
to pay me, I hope you're listening,
twice: that's once for the shares I own, and once

for what the government takes from you.

I'd feel a lot sorrier about this situation
except if you're like almost everybody I've ever worked with,
instead of being enraged at losing this much of
the value of what our work creates each week
—without anybody even inquiring
if we suckers agree to the donation,
let alone anyone announcing *Gosh, I'm sure grateful*
for your contribution to
my personal bag of gold,
a bunch of us dream of becoming a boss, too
—soaking up sixteen, or a hundred and sixty, times
as much every month as the rest of those employed here.
And another pile of us
claim we don't want the responsibility
—*It's the company's worry* or *Close enough for government work*—
but want to get rich anyway:
blowing plenty on lotteries, Vegas twice a year
or at one of the new Indian casinos.
Worse, due to some amazing sleight-of-hand
on the part of the financial institutions
now everybody who has two dollars to rub together
is busy stealing from every other Mr. and Mrs. Schmuck
who drags herself or himself to the job each morning.
Some genius suggested to the bank executives:
Boys, let's forget being a depository:
investing the smelly people's miserable savings
and paying out a guaranteed interest on their pittances.
To hell with 'em. It's time we banks stopped being
Mr. Nice Guy. Let the rubes invest their own damn money.
Thus the mutual fund was spawned
and the retirement plan based on such genteel roulette
so each of us is scrabbling to pick up
bucks we didn't earn
groping deep in that magical fog known as
capitalism, a mist dripping with money for you and me
that will never dissipate, that will last

a thousand years. Even down at the union office,
first thing in the morning everyone is cracking open the paper
to find their stocks, to learn how much
they made yesterday off other people's labor.

Yeah, it's crazy, it's the end of the week, payday,
and I say: thanks,
gals and guys; don't think
I don't appreciate it.

THE ORDER IN WHICH WE DO THINGS

Was not established by God
Only infrequently has a biological basis
Follows designated procedures or assembly instructions

Displays significant influence of parental models
Reflects our current personal values and priorities
Was determined by a team of consultants

Indicates our choice of who to please
Derives from a self-established estimate of the best use of our time or
    other resources
Does not always correspond to company policy

Is organized from easiest to most difficult, or vice versa
Is organized from most to least likely to generate rewards, or vice versa
Differs from the wording of the collective agreement

If consistently adhered to becomes routine, or obsessive
Demonstrates functionality of memory
Originates as a consequence of the foreman's mood on a given morning

Can have an historical provenance, including the production of an
    apparently random list
Arises from the need to placate or neutralize a controlling hierarchy
Represents a helpful factor in econometric analysis

Is who
We are

WHAT YOU'LL FIND WHEN YOU GET AHEAD

is a lot of people already there.
And they aren't the least bit happy
about your presence

                because they liked it fine
before you showed up:
newcomers always change matters for the worse.
Also, if enough men and women such as you
appear, this location won't remain ahead
but revert to being a place no different from
where the current inhabitants originated.
So they're not a welcoming group,
to put it mildly. Which forces you to act just as nasty
if you don't already
in order to hang on to your new address.
This mean-spiritedness
is an inescapable aspect of getting ahead.

                      As an alternative
how about striving for an advance
shared by everyone
or as many people as is possible
—given the effects of childhood malnutrition,
seriously dysfunctional parents,
or in general being a biological or social loser
at life's lottery?
For when most of us benefit
as a consequence of one person's bright idea
or a surge of common effort,
the reality is acknowledged
that no matter how much John or Joan plays the hermit,
the self-sufficient loner,
they, and we, live in an interactive community
which accounts for why
willingly, or under the duress of money,

roads get paved and repaired,
bagels are baked and
wholesaled to the local stores,
you can go downtown and find a dentist.

                                    Every other view
of ourselves
is an illusion—not that fantasies don't provide
an efficacious framework
for as long as women and men believe in them strongly.
But me-apart-from-everybody-else, me-against-
everybody-else, is a kind of psychosomatic illness:
a mass- or minority-hysteria
that dissipates under the beady eye of reason,
once such can be brought to bear.

                              Even Henry Ford
who hated unions, Jews, you name it,
had the idea that if he paid the people who built his cars
a wage of a size to ensure they could afford to buy the product,
he'd sell far more than if he dispensed
a subsistence level of remuneration
—thus limiting demand for his machines to
that tiny bunch of folks
who officially had elbowed past the ruck.

                                  This single thought
of his
helped propel capitalism happily onwards another century
and more. Of course Mr. Ford didn't want to see his employees
prosperous, but merely with income to dispose
in his direction. Yet how weird that someone with his attitudes
should have had even a small part
of the right idea.

                        Meantime, we who do not decree our paycheques
clock on, sign in, or otherwise arrive at work
and by this act and the next eight hours

ensure a handful of people do better than ourselves. Seems backwards
to me, since the particular ordinary tasks
of nearly everyone
jointly heave this world around.

                                    And consider the science,
the geometry,
of this arrangement:
there's really no way to outdistance others
on a spherical rotating planet,
try as you might: the Audrey and Ernie you regard as
trailing you
inexorably attain the spot you occupy now
within a few hours. Though you can imagine yourself
perpetually in front,
if a single person who lags after
should look to the rear in search of the big picture,
and especially if enough of the also-rans glance back
to try to puzzle out their situation,
they'll observe that you,
along with each individual convinced
he or she has gotten ahead,
are in fact following behind
where the rest of us are employed all day,
where everybody truly is.

THE ROAD FATHER

NINETEEN NINETY-NINE

High winter in Paulson Pass:
spruce and fir on the slopes are tightly wrapped by snow
that shapes these conifers into white spires
rising from drifts.
The blue sky over the peaks, banked snow along the road,
and the snowy highway itself
pulse under a January sun's
crisp inundation of light.

                Then a figure
stands in the white road: white trousers,
khaki sweater and balaclava
and the black stick of a slung rifle.
He lifts the palm of a glove toward my truck
as I approach. I observe a similar young man
on the highway beyond him
who faces the opposite direction. As I slow,
the opening of a forest road emerges,
choked now with a line of large, dark-green, heavy vehicles
pointed toward me, each bearing
a tiny representation of the flag of this country
above the grille. On the churned snow
around the stalled convoy
dozens of other men cluster, each with an FN
held in his hand
or suspended from a shoulder.

                My engine slows to idle;
the soldier in front of me
shouts something I can't hear
at the troop on the side road.
A reply is aimed at him
and he impatiently waves me past.

                Behind me the trucks of war

perhaps will enter the highway
or initiate a different aspect of their operational plans
this day in the bright alpine.

As a thousand years
of human blood staining snow
and pooling on soil, cloth, flesh
near an end, after forty more generations
of our killing our own species
have been endured,
the survivors are training hard.
Weapons, transport, tactics
tested and functional in any climate,
every terrain, we ready our children
to manufacture
the next century of death.

ON EBY'S PATH

a shortcut between Fourth and Third Avenues East,
Prince Rupert, B.C.

Odor of earth
soaked nearly black
and of a snarled weave of green
that clambers up from wet ground:
salmonberry, its fruit still emerald buds;
cow parsnip, hoisting white floral umbrellas;
devil's club; horsetail fern; wild rose.

Forty years previously, a boy
crouched at the edge of this trail
and of others that snuck through the dripping town.
The coarse green aroma, these spiny growths
were my companions, siblings
—like myself, newly arrived
in this settlement, existing
on the margins of houses and streets,
yet who thrived in the spaces
unintentionally left for us.

In my presence, my absence, the underbrush
forces its way toward the light:
grey clouds that lower over this muskeg shelf
by the grey sea. A prickly exuberance
ignorant and fertile, endures,
resists each attempt to chop it back,
claims its bequest.

These fellow sojourners
comfort me: another 12-year-old
will pause alone on a muddy path
to inhale a saturated foliage, bristly stalks,

the hush of rain on wide leaves.
My dreams began here
in water transformed to slow green flames
from which drifts a fecund stench of
soil, stem, blossom.
This verdancy that presses forward
is a child of those who constructed my imagination
—as I am: their persistence
testimony to
the inexorable solidarity of life.

THE ROAD FATHER

In the middle of the afternoon
the shadows of the tops of the pines
this highway races through
stretch across the gravel shoulder
and touch the asphalt's edge.
Since morning I have wound along a river valley
or accelerated up the slopes of a range
and the sounds of tires on pavement,
of metal and glass being forced through air,
of the steady engine
have repeated:

Let the young man go.
Let him veer away, pass you, fall behind
—the youth you were, who set out thirty years ago
to cross the uncertainties
of his days, hands on the wheel,
and loved this voyaging: its anxieties and achievements,
new country rising into view
or drifting by in the ebb and flow
of terrestrial tides, loved the solitude
—his voice lifted into song
that blended with the noises of the motor,
his evenings at a campfire close by the cooling car,
near a stream heard for a single night.

Let him go: you will still pursue
delights these roads urge you toward.
But what the young man seeks
are not the goals you search for
as the land flattens into fields,
cattle begin grazing, rolls of hay cure
under a summer sun.

He will travel safely, safer than a child,

because wherever he ventures
he can only end here, behind this wheel you hold.
So let him run: in the joy and terror of his age
he has other maps to consult, other routes
to power down. You will feel no less exultant
to pull into the suburbs of someplace
after a long haul; you can even meet him
from time to time, laugh over coffees
taken outside to drink standing beside your vehicles,
describing the crazy van driver who overtook you,
a shortcut that got you snared in two-lane traffic,
and listening to his own tales—bonded with him by the love
of the road, yet each of you with
a different distance to cover.

                    My tires
cut across the trees' full shadows now,
ears pulsing with the highway's
rhythms, its
plea or command:
Let the young man go

WHAT THE SIXTIES MEAN TO ME

"It's winter in America."

—Gil Scott-Heron

In *The Elegant Universe*, 1999,
Brian Greene explains that to harmonize
quantum mechanics and Einstein's special relativity,
and to ensure the equations involved
do not generate the meaninglessness of
negative probability values,
string theory posits
that besides the three spatial
and one temporal dimensions of our accustomed existence,
an additional seven infinitesimal dimensions
are compressed throughout the universe.

Thus at each location and moment
immense possibilities we can scarcely conceptualize
let alone traverse, depict or experience,
are seeded, coiled, poised.

Further, some scientists suggest
that of the seven unknown facets of the cosmos
some may be minuscule time dimensions
folded into the spatial fabric,
potentially directing time's flow not only backwards
but also toward unimaginable other orientations,
velocities, shapes.

So I have to stress that the Sixties
occurred in the Fifties
—the pervasive texture of parking meters, laundromats,
front stoops, canned peas
and stained paper. Despite how hindsight measures
and interprets the ominipresent background radiation,

what happened to some other people and I
during and against a different era

was as if all that wraps tightly, invisibly
about and within us
uncurled for a day, a month, longer,
and we tasted colors in the ordinary air
and watched sounds
whose vibrations were vivid and sweet as
those of some previously-unencountered spectrum of energy
whose pulses we had no syllables to name,
only register in awe,
that generate in each observer of their crackling beauty
new senses with which to apprehend
more than such surges:
a separate world

and which encouraged us also to trace repeatedly
every letter of *justice*
with clumsy fingers, urgent
fingers, with fists, rocks,
iron rods
and naked words.

Our days
resembled a fresh season: at once a cornucopia,
a magician's hat, and
an M-16 barrel
—beneficent, foolish, cynical, threatened.
No dawn was safe from sunset;
no pleasure less than sky.
I never remember being sad.
Leaf after leaf, road upon road
shimmered for me; I had not known
there could be this much planet
and from the cries on every side
I deduced others were equally startled.

We pushed through the huge gelatinous hours
slowly, as though weighted: each inch of skin
was processing electromagnetic fields
of an hitherto-unacknowledged type
released by our acquisition of the expanded dimensions.
A door opened, then opened and
opened—became a fissure in stone, a
canyon, a valley of scented lupine,
fireweed, pearly everlasting, then
wider, a plain with
bougainvillea, lemon, the thick haze of
eucalyptus, until
tectonic plates
heaved further apart.
Only the intense attention
of the police
and their money
could bar the route to
that untried continent, claw down the weak
and stupid of our migration,
frighten us, constrict us, double us back
in order
through an interstice.

To have found under the asphalt,
the beach, taught us what no doubter could believe:
the difficult mathematics
of the visible world,
as well as to exult
with love when our common life
once more gains any access
to the hidden geometries
—cosmometries, really—
of wonder. Like veterans of
peril in war or
nature, we tumbled through a series of instants
that reconfigured forever—despite any subsequent
individual failure to thrive—

what we understand
about November, about
May.

IN MEMORY OF A. W. PURDY

(d. Apr. 2000)

I

Death came for him in the Spring:
a dark crocus.
For even Winter, that emblem of
age and aridity,
sickens and dies
and by that act nurtures
a different season. The snow, the crocuses
appear and vanish repeatedly:
the spinning biosphere they help form
is bound in turn to a rotating planet
—on which Al Purdy lived once
and just once.

Sid Marty phoned
from his ranch up Willow Valley Road
in the Alberta foothills
to let me know.
"*All* the fathers are dying," I responded
—my own father, exhausted to the core by a hospital's
intrusive and agonizing procedures
to restore one collapsed bodily system after another,
had convinced his doctors the previous May to grant
the peace of the hospice ward
in which he could sleep his solitary way out of the world.
"This point in our lives," I told Marty,
"must have happened to our fathers, also."

"We've been able to paddle around,"
Marty mused, "in the shallows
as long as they were beyond us out in the open ocean.
Now we have to voyage

where they went, onto deep water."

And I remembered a poem by Earle Birney,
Purdy's old colleague, now lost as him under the long swells
of the expanse with no further shore: *That sea
is hight Time,*
Birney wrote, adopting an archaic tongue,
we drift to map's end.

II

Purdy shambled across the earth, a big man
whose hands en route pushed at a taxi meter, at
pens, at newly manufactured mattresses,
used books, typewriters, the edges of lecterns,
case after case of beer.
As he travelled, he delighted in
the contours of the landscape,
its swales and bluffs, ridges and
hollows. He marvelled, too,
at much he discovered among this geology:
electrical switchyards, grainfields, magistrate's courtrooms
and the men and women who inhabit each region or district,
with their dogs, flower beds, rusted-out cars.

On everything Purdy loved most
he bestowed
the name of his country.
Yet he was wrong.
In the forest that straddles the border here, the firs
on each side do not clutch
differing small flags in their twigs.
The Great Divide, as mapmakers understand,
occurs along another line.
Still, Purdy did not know what else to do
with his huge affection for all he encountered.
He gazed at what pleased him
with the proprietary eyes

of pure joy. He called it *Canada*, but
it was Purdy.

III

Now the poet lives in his words, which
as Purdy himself would note,
is a damn strange constricted airless waterless
place to live
—no rhubarb pies or Molson's Ale,
no girls in their flirty summer tops.

And any language can die, or change shape
until only pedants and their victims
are able to drudge through it:
maybe one in ten thousand of these
feels the neuron's spark of wit in a phrase
or description regarded as ironic or humorous by a former time.

Yet those weakest of constructs—words, poems—
have endured centuries
so far, which given the track record of
most things humans create and believe in
isn't shabby at all. So perhaps some of Purdy's words
will stumble a little tipsily into the future

viewing wonders—and possibly horrors—he now
won't be able to see for himself.
His gift to me
was his rambling: his itinerant lines and
peripatetic stanzas—apparently relaxed, inquisitive, opinionated,
exactly like someone talking:

a conversation with the reader so cunningly shaped
that the choice of structure or other artistic details
is not the point of the piece, any more than a news story
reveals its architecture. His boozy self-confidence

took poetry to a place nobody else had been.
Who cares? you say. I care,

and maybe the eons will. If not, his life and achievements
were no less futile than those of the rest of us.
I drive back from town on an asphalt road
dry in the middle of the lanes now that the rain has passed.
Over my truck's speakers
I hear a guitar chord struck,

then a second one, and a human voice
begins to chant a story,
singing me home.
Purdy wasn't a singer, even if a fan or reviewer
occasionally waxed rhetorical.
But when he depressed a key

and the shaft lifted and fell toward the paper,
that passage of metal through air vibrated like
two people who argue in bed or
in a bar, a coyote taunting the Valley dogs,
the raucous blast of a diesel train engine
that approaches a crossing, a class of grade twos

squawking their version of anybody's national anthem,
a bellow from a steer in Kooznetsoff's field
along the Lower Road, wind
swooping over tundra.
And since Al Purdy was at ease
with the currents and rollers of Time

I'll add that the sound
was whatever noise dinosaurs uttered
in an amorous mood, the skritch-skritch of a quill pen,
a choir in full flight during a requiem mass
(okay, maybe he did sing a little),
a black crocus breaking through soil

into the light of day.

GOD HATES HAIR

Most interpreters of the divine concur
—No matter how much they denounce
Their colleagues' teachings on every other matter—
God hates hair.
Temples, cathedrals
And even holy policy manuals for daily living
Insist God desires a screen of cloth be placed
Between the thatch on the human skull
And the Creator's all-seeing Eye.
We are informed that a beanie, a scarf,
Or an entire bathmat
Must ride atop the head
Lest the Maker catch a glimpse of
The pile of extruded threads
He evidently regards with repugnance.

The assumption of the clerics appears to be
God is a failed hairdresser
Or barber, or that His own hair
Has fallen out: so many sects and cults
Shave the pate to indicate obedience to the Sacred Will
Or at the very least proffer a plate-sized dome
Ringed by a fringe of benighted matter
Like a tabernacle rising in the midst of Gomorrah.

If we follow these dictates to their logical end
Men who naturally become bald should be acclaimed
The most blessed and saintly among us.
Indeed, given women's proclivity toward hair
No wonder not a single faith exalts women
—Except the religions women start themselves.
And surely the manufacturers and sellers of toupees
Must be counted the worst blasphemers on the planet
For encouraging the faithful
To acquire and flaunt what God has decreed abhorrent.

Also, God's preference for short-haired goats
Over wooly sheep
Makes sense. Yet why are so few mammals He invented
Entirely hairless? Why are the plains
Covered in flowing grasses
And the mountains and river-valleys
Tufted with trees?

I hope all the proclamations and edicts
Issued by the pious
Are not based on a Cosmic misunderstanding
Or mistranslation: that it will turn out to be fingernails
God wants removed or covered
—Or maybe elbows, earlobes,
Or no part of our body—
To indicate belief in His everlasting Glory and Might
And of course that of His local representatives.

BIG WEATHER

My delight is to be
out on the highway
in big weather:
cresting a hill to suddenly overlook
a steep drop the route hairpins down
to a crossroads hamlet, like a toy village, far below.
For this instant, I'm at the same height as a huge cumulus
suspended above the wooded valleys,
the March sky here all sun and floating islands,
cloudbergs, of inflated white.

                    My truck today
is riding the stormtrack
east—striking the mountain walls and then lifting
through the passes,
gathering moisture again from the rivers and lakes
and the unbroken slopes of conifers exhaling
thousand of litres of water an hour skyward.
So a drizzle begins as another range approaches
and then rain floods down as my tires
start the long climb to the summit of
the gap between these peaks.

And in the troughs of the valleys
gusts of wind quarter my vehicle:
suspended highway signs swing out
nearly parallel to the ground
and flags are torn half away
where they ripple loudly from poles around the
canyon motel cafe general store.

                    Even the light
travels through this afternoon of small rain
and vibrant air: high wisps of cirrus float over
until fifty kilometres later I steer beneath

a dark wet lid of nimbostratus
that soon transforms into lucent blue, the asphalt now damp
and the roadside roofs steaming

                      before I ascend the face
of a pine ridge
and roll across tableland where snow is banked
in strips over the fields, earth
newly uncovered in swirls and pools between the drifts,
the soil pallid and dusty
as it awaits more pungent weather
that will, like me,
arrive and pass on.

HIDDEN MOUNTAIN

ON PERRY RIDGE

I strode up into my woods
on an autumn noon
past the fringe of glowing alder and maple
into the more sombre rooms of cedar, pine, fir
—although amid the evergreens,
pillars of luminous birch
and the yellowing larch
shone, and the rough paths I followed
were mottled by rivers of fluorescent leaves
wind-drifted down from these beacons.

As I scrambled higher and paced
the steep tangle of the ridge
I frightened two brown deer
and was shocked in turn
by the sudden flight of a grouse,
despite how I whistled and sang
while I climbed, wary of the bear
—dark menace—I knew also claimed this slope
I struggled to ascend
without a goal
other than to indulge an exuberant blue sky

until where my boots displaced the forest duff
or found purchase on black soil,
beneath the thrust of my passage
I felt a gleam burst out
as if the stones and brush and trees of this hill
were a thin veneer over
an incandescence, the surface of a sphere
which radiated a sentient and ecstatic fire
that imbued this hour, and anyone who passed,
with the incendiary force
of another, hidden mountain.

THE BLOSSOMING

> *. . . I realize*
> *That if I stepped out of my body I would break*
> *Into blossom.*

—James Wright

Icy air
drawn sweet into my nose and throat
as my skis pump and glide
tracking the valley

between spruce and fir, some cedar where a creek
trickles past humped white cornices
banked on either side of its flow.
And the cold on my face

increases as I pole and sway
out of the woods onto an unsheltered
white meadow or marsh
open to the wind

so the wax under my boards
stutters a little in the increased coolness
and then breaks smooth again
where the trail returns to the forest.

But as I steadily traverse a straight run
sheltered by evergreens on one hand
and on the other an unbroken expanse
above a pond,

   a red-gold ovoid
expands within my chest
to fill the body cavity: I sense the rounded surface inside me
layered with glowing leaves

like scales, or overlapping
feathers, or small gilded ruddy plates
of armor. The ovate object
transmits, incarnates, an exultant

happiness: not sensual but kinetic,
an ecstasy of motion,
of function.
This delight is the pleasure

provided to an angel by
its body: nothing of soul
but the blessing of
an unearthly corporality

suspended now within me
—a ring of petals
merged tightly around their core,
a taut mass, with short tendril-like extensions

that insinuate their way
into my four oscillating limbs.
This manifestation proposes
the flesh of a peach

—that sweet, sun-warmed, juicy pulp—
were desiccated, wooden,
compared to the teeming fluid miracle
of its stone.

FEAR ECLIPSED BY DISTANCE

i

In March flood, the river
braids and churns down Upper Falls
from bank to bank around Havermale Island
Viewed from the footbridge
the torrent is a pillar of cloud choked with death
surging at me

—oblivion incarnate: a pulsing, whitish-brown fire
that lunges my direction

Yet under the bridge's downstream railing
the flow's power recedes
intact but used: the wake of a huge ship

ii

Above the eastern hills
the moon
accepts the earth's shadow
between its legs

Moment by moment
the curved intrusion dulls
the lunar glare

reducing our companion stone
to an edge of light
that blurs the outline of a disk

as though we are not propelled by
a star
that does not spin through a galaxy
that does not hurtle outwards

—as if our planet
had fashioned
roots

iii

When electricity fails
here in the country
the face of my clock
blackens
Once current is restored

red numbers flash repeatedly
to signal the commencement of the universe
—and something wrong
with time

Until then, clusters of candles
a kerosene lamp
shadow my house

the wood in the basement furnace
creaks and spits

This is how we lived
for generations since we occupied
this globe

In the sweet-smelling dark
the future is hidden

by ridges and swales
down whose contours pour
the terror that beckons the night
inside me, as though
to welcome the bridegroom, the stranger, the
guest

FOR BILL SUTHERLAND (1919-1997)

1

Ragged streamers of geese
pump over the December freeway
in central Oregon, bearing east above the sawmills
at the river's edge

Later more geese in Washington
vee north across the sky as the freeway cuts
through dry hills, powdered with snow

A moon two days shy of full
lifts
directly where the road aims ahead

2

It is lonely without God
We exist as someone
who has moved to a new town
The inhabitants appear foreign, reserved
We are uncertain which hardware store is best
or who stocks familiar brands of food
We are gripped with longing for how we lived before
—the men and women we encountered on the street
who knew us, the ease with which we absorbed
the locale's services and institutions
We forget the group of merchants in a cafe
plotting, the smirk of meanness
as one raises her coffee cup
We overlook the teacher arrested
for years of interference with children, the woman
ostensibly killed in a trailer fire
whose autopsy revealed she had been strangled

In this new place, the municipal parks are empty
except for frozen underbrush
The avenues are not kept plowed—
drifts of slush are permitted to clump and congeal
Yet we know why we relocated here
Our children will find this geography
the ease and warmth of home

3

Your daughter crouches alone, crumpled and sobbing
at one end of your coffin
as the moon rises above the snowfield
smudged by an overcast

Your huge box is still suspended above ground
on straps secured to the temporary chrome frame
Snow is mounded on three sides of
what will be your grave

The only light is a single candle
a mourner fastened in a snowbank
beside your daughter's cries of dizzying
unredeemable pain

The funeral party with its drums and bagpipes
has vanished, except for two vehicles of her friends
who cluster some distance away
and gaze at the austere night hillside

The Legion has left a flag on your coffin
Over it, her moans escape to the vacant branches of trees
like breath
like geese, that shiver high in the cold air

toward water

SOARING CROW

Before you fear death
consider—what if death did not work?
A vanity of crows
lifts argumentatively from branches
of an alder—one black form
pulses slowly overhead
its wings creaking against air,
another relocates the valley's thermals
and coasts like an osprey out over the river.

Death defunct,
vanished. What would be left behind
as death's will, death's estate?
The aged who have outlived themselves
—who recognize no one,
who we call by another person's name:
these beings, old since rebirth,
living and living. And the woods crowded:
too many siskins, coyote, shrews.
The land along the highway teeming
with trucks, housetrailers winched into fields
down newly-bulldozed laneways,
straw-colored skeletons of homes
taking shape in each meadow, going up.
Everything going higher:
prices, knapweed, skyscrapers
—no death to calm us down,
straighten us out, start
from square one. No square one.
The soaring crow peers around at it all,
paroled from death, forever
unleashed.

THE ANTI-PROMETHEUS

Afterwards, when I have taken the light
the world will have to function
with this deficiency

like a landscape encountered by night:
the corn growing in the invisible fields
beside houses where the furniture and crockery
hover in rooms of black solitude
and the scent of marigolds as you lean over a bed

or, if you are driving, graders,
excavators and other heavy equipment
loom paralyzed from time to time
along the shoulder
as do small files of tractor-trailers.
Only the stars evince
scattered recurring memories of day.

Except that not stillness but
our entire intricate flourishing,
each of our errors and triumphs,
will have to occur without the sun.
A cow must be secured
to the milking device, and the machines
collect and prepare the fluid for delivery
to the processor, who needs to have previously stocked
containers printed and coated ready to be filled.
The distributor must make his rounds to the huge groceterias
and the corner stores, so that yet other hands can touch
the product, later withdrawing it from a refrigerator
to pour into a glass

                    —all without light.
Much can adapt,
and new things will be created

and expand under these conditions, things
that would have been better had I not taken with me
the fire. But I will,
and ever afterwards this world
must endure the dark
as best it can.

MOVING TO HEAVEN

Perhaps it's month end: on the freeway
amid the usual cars, delivery vans,
and tractor-trailers,
flows an irregular stream of pickups
crammed with old sofas, televisions, mattresses,
ironing boards, with a plastic tarp over everything
half worked free from its tie-downs, flapping,
and of sedans, back seats heaped with stereo equipment, skis,
lamps, that tow u-built trailers
laden with cardboard boxes of irregular shapes and conditions,
piled around rolled rugs, chairs, kids' bicycles,
and a refrigerator perilously secured by vinyl ropes.
Also present are two-vehicle convoys
overtaken by most other traffic:
a rental van proceeding stolidly with a male behind the wheel,
followed obediently by a car driven by a female,
rear seat jammed with more containers, framed art,
and potted ferns.

As the border approaches, the landscape
alters. Since morning the road has emerged
from a forest of cedar and fir and alder,
with thick undergrowth on steep mountain walls,
into an open flatness: vistas of arid sage
that extend to every horizon. When the route climbs,
small stands of pine cluster near the highway,
the trees at last merging into woods
that nudge up to the road's paved shoulder.
Even the sky has simplified:
a low grey mat of nimbostratus
starts to disperse over the dry lands
while the air brightens
to a faultless clarity.

A succession of signboards

announce the line. Traffic thins to
a chain of packed vehicles that gears down
to traverse sets of rumble strips
and pulls up to the bumper of a sedan or pickup halted
in front, everyone's engines pulsating.

A structure shimmers ahead in the exhaust.
The vehicles fan out along marked lanes
leading to one of a row of booths.
When the machines reach the booth's window
each driver is required to make a declaration:

What are you carrying with you?
Any emotions or physical possessions
you intend to bring here?
What do you plan to do
during your stay?
No one is certain which items or activities
are prohibited; every driver has prepared answers
according to the best information he or she could glean.
Rumors persist of unexpected questions
whose purpose is not evident: *Were you ever*
arrested? Have you exhibited cruelty
toward another life-form?
Should a person be completely honest
even at the risk of misinterpretation?
Or are there preferred responses?

In one section of the lineup,
a sagging trailer in front of a woman
lurches forward a car-length
and then stops once more. Through her windshield,
the woman believes she glimpses
far past the structures that bar her way
a range of hills, mottled dun and blue.

ICE LAKE

Again I have been brought
to a small snowbound lake, at the close
of afternoon

that stretches to a shore of fir and cedar or pine
The air has thickened: a few snowflakes
precipitate out and float

but the place
vibrates with import
for me, an event

of huge significance
struggles to occur
Clumps of snow

drape around the protruding soil and rocks
of the forest's
gullies and banks

The wind mutters its uninterpretable credo
in the evergreen branches
Perhaps this lake, or one it resembles

is where my husk will be placed
to return to earth
below a stone

Or the locale
is a communication
a power wishes me to hear

While a child, I was taken to skate
on a pond like this
I recall how at the furthest edge of ice

a creek pushed through the green wall of the wood
and I desired to trace, to drift up that frozen path
into the shadowed wildness

More recently, I skied a valley
to reach the expanse of a wider lake
and stare across, below white peaks

This vision of
a dimming day, trees, and stilled water
rises repeatedly into my path

although years can speed between the moments
I feel unmistakably the prescient scene
urges me to wait in the cold air

as for a change of season
a mystery
I am destined to encounter and endure

CIRCLE

Chill March night.
Directly overhead,
framed by the west ridge, the high firs
to the south
and the Valley's east wall,
a half moon

burns, while around it, some distance out
among the scattered stars,
an immense ring
glows:
ice crystals in the atmosphere
illuminated into wonder.

Who could be shown
too many gifts like these? This is why
I do not want to end.
Yet the firs
will outlast me.
When I have evaporated,
another person on this spot will gaze up
at the moon encircled, or won't.

My only solace
is that I stood here,
that I will no longer watch
but form part of
the lit darkness, burning cold.
I will be in and of
the beautiful night.

RIG

When new, a tractor and semi-trailer,
or a train of tractor, semi-, and full trailer,
function as one: the conscious intelligence
in the cab, and heavy rolling warehouses linked behind,
meld into a single supple rig.

                              As they age, however,
anything that is joined to the tractor
—low beds, flat beds, belly-dumpers—
begins to diverge in intention
from what directs where the unit travels,
the contracts it undertakes.

                    Tires wear
and suddenly disintegrate, brake lines crack
and need replacement, the steady scuff of the road
chips slowly at the trailers' undercarriages and sides.
The tractor undergoes its own weathering
and, in addition, the weight of the sagging burden it pulls
season after season, midnights and early afternoons,
tugs continually at its frame. Microscopic stress fractures
form and propagate.

Yet the bruteness of what was designed
only to bear, to transport,
decays quicker than the tractor's intricate electronics,
its steering mechanisms, grilledenser.
At last, on a shameful slope, some grit next to a spinning shaft,
or a seized brake, or a weighted axle
that surged over a frost heave
and collapsed, brings the rig
to the edge of the road, still.

Ahead could lie a tow, repairs,
and more years of hauling past prospects of Spring hay

lifting under the sweep of irrigation water
with forested hills beyond staking the valley rim.
And of congestion in both lanes that spreads back up the line,
slowing the torrent of vehicles to a walk, then a stop
until five long miles further the obstruction dissolves
for no obvious reason. But this moment
at the shoulder, the engine
idling, or shut down, the buckled tilt to the trailer
an instant's curiosity to everyone wheeling by,
could be the start of the end: the driver
sick of the aggravation, one more manifestation of trouble
from an aged rig, decides to pack it in forever.

Or more determinedly,
the fault in the trailer occurring at high speed,
the load shifting, overturning the unit,
the entire train on its side, toppled into scrap metal and
pools of leaked fluids
in a roadside gully.

              Self and soul, body and mind
are indistinguishable in the flashing lights of
emergency crews, flares and cones set out,
a patrolman waving traffic on
until the wreckers appear and begin their scavenging.
Afterwards, under great clouds that reveal and mask the sun
the lanes rise and descend through the cut
without comment, as in the flow of traffic
an empty flatbed speeding home
signals behind a tall load of logs, and pulls around.

CANS OF NAILS

WHAT A WORD LACKS

Wind pushing against the serifs
or other surfaces of its letters

Desire for fame
A molar sensitive to chewing gum

Memory of a sentence
the word recently participated in

whose succinctness was especially pleasing
A list of several phone calls to complete

one of which the word dreads making
A business plan that includes

a cash flow projection
after three months, six months and a year

Terror at the thought of self-annihilation
that will come with the word's

eventual extinction
Dreams in which the word murders another

with a gun, and then tries to flee
by clambering down the outside of a multistory building

Regret at not stepping forward
to take its rightful place in a phrase

because the word did not feel welcome
Groceries to purchase, including white wine and dishcloths

Hair growing

on many parts of its skin

Fear of spiders, dogs
or the moon

A MEETING WITH NERUDA IN TORONTO

Last August, I watched Pablo Neruda
on the patio of the Bloor Street Diner
—which is neither a diner nor on Bloor Street
but rather a French restaurant on Bay,
that being how it is with names on this planet.
Neruda was seated
two tables from me, eating supper with a woman about his age,
late sixties I would guess. They seemed to be gently celebrating
some event, working through a bottle of white wine
kept chilled in a small pail perched on a stand
from which at intervals
the poet would decorously refill both glasses.
The man was unmistakably Neruda,
though he had been dead for twenty-five years
and eleven months: he was portly, with large bald head
that rose egg-shaped above his eyelashes and eyes
that were at once hooded, tender
and ablaze with an intense curiosity, a fascination
with whatever his face pointed them at,
so they absorbed and embraced
the clatter of the patrons jammed around him
in this establishment perched just over the sidewalk
of a busy street shadowed by immense office towers.
Yet a distance was in his gaze, too:
that of a traveller savoring a moment
in the midst of a culture very different from his own,
or that of a storyteller aware he intends to later narrate
the amusing dimensions of even a delightful repast
or hotel accommodation, a famous natural feature or
exhibit at a renowned art gallery
or anthropological museum.

                Mostly, though,
the poet stared at his companion, probably Mathilde,
his last wife. When he spoke to her, or she spoke,

his eyes held such a loving, solicitous,
—dare I suggest, uxorious—aspect
that the two seemed tented within
a nimbus of tenderness
startling in this era of omnipresent and accelerated
conjugal decay.
Her back was to me, where I shovelled down pasta
but I observed how they delicately handed across
bread or certain spices that the other wished, and how
each appeared transfixed by the beloved's face
as they talked quietly together—I could not hear
over the traffic noise and
the patio's chatter and rattle of utensils
if they addressed one another in Spanish or in English—
or each stared silently at the other
above raised chalices of wine.

                              Occasionally Neruda's glance
swept about the place. Strangest to me, however,
is that from time to time his face turned
in my direction. His eyes when they met mine
were simultaneously shy, thoughtful and self-assured
as though he knew me from somewhere
and was considering addressing me, perfectly at ease
with my uncertainty about who he might be,
the way in my town in the mountains
people I don't know in stores or on the street
—strangers I recognize
from years of encountering them at children's concerts, or
in service or retail capacities,
or at the park—will regard me and comment
on the unusual flooding this Spring, or some local news
like a recent power outage or tragic avalanche,
or a focus of the moment—
perhaps another customer who has left behind her credit card,
or been rude, or is pluckily dealing with a physical affliction.
In this manner, Neruda gazed steadily at me
and I could not interpret with any assurance

what he wished to communicate. For a second,
I would conclude his eyes meant to indicate
This is how to live: a cherished wife
who is also a sweet companion
and compañero, seated before a tasty clam linguine
with a good Chardonnay. Or some cast to his face
convinced me his eyes meant to silently encourage me
I, too, have had ups and downs
as a writer. Keep practicing your art:
what you are driven to utter
is needed, while neglect or hostility
are in some measure every author's lot.
Then I would be certain
his message was *I am aware you have diligently enjoyed*
much of my work in translation—I don't translate well
into English, but let that pass—
and I would be pleased to converse with you,
except that such an exchange is impossible,
given my present circumstances,
being dead. Rather let me model for you
an energetic and pleasantly-rewarded middle age.
Each instance our eyes connected
mine would slip away first
and when I swung back he would be deep in communion
with his tablemate.

               Before the group I was with
started to ingest the pastries we had ordered for dessert
Neruda and Mathilde rose to leave.
As they approached our table I saw clearly
the person who had enraptured the poet
and thought how ordinary she appeared
as most of us do, except when viewed through the lens
of heightened emotions. Neruda looked straight at me
one final time as he passed
before the couple vanished toward the clump of patrons
waiting at the cashier's station. A wine bottle

stood drained on their table for a minute.
Then a waitress and busboy descended
and speedily erased the poet's presence, setting out
fresh cloth napkins, cutlery, and water tumblers
and then dashing to the next chore,
so, in a few seconds, the place
where the poet and his wife had been
was left prepared
but vacant.

AT DUSK, THE DEER MOVE TO WATER

The words
hover, veer, tumble
aloft
in the space where the four spheres
overlap:
inner, exterior, day, darkness

Southeast of Paulson Pass,
as the highway twists down through the wooded canyons
a Spring grove of aspen, cottonwood, alder,
flashes
a shimmering green and yellow cloud
and my spirit exults

at the leaves telling
a name of this world
—this world of names recounted
in a single
unnameable
word

while above the shining name
where the four expanses merge,
entwine (though four
is neither their measure
nor number) a solitary
crow
hangs on the thermals
wings stretched wide like a hawk
or eagle
tilting, teetering on the rising air
that pours up from creekbed,
slope of fir and pine
and the route I follow through the trees—
the dark road

that closes toward,
then turns from
the light

TWO POETS I ADMIRE CONTACT ME ON THE SAME DAY

From the eastern foot of the Crowsnest Pass
Sid Marty telephones: *Plant a flower for me*
in your Grave of Literary Ambition
—the bed of annuals I gave that name
in my front meadow.
He has two new books about to appear,
still not enough money, but when he writes

aspen bluffs take shape in my mind.
I hear the shuffling and reshuffling
of the small spade-shaped leaves in a wind,
the crackle of a yearling brown bear
moving amid last autumn's deadfalls
and the cry of woodland birds
deep in the grove: cedar waxwing, flicker, chickadee.

And a letter arrives
from Peter Christensen's acreage
on Redstreak Mountain above Radium
at the Rockies' western edge,
sentences that apologize, sort of,
for him accidentally nudging his pickup into the cribwork
of a raised flowerbed attached to my house
and skewing the whole construction
as he departed after some hours we spent drinking
when he showed unexpectedly one day last October.

His envelope also contains
a poem of his about finding one of my books
in a backcountry bookstore.
Mine is the only collection of poems in the shop,
he explains, and he decides not to buy the volume
because if he did

it would be as if there were no poetry.

These mountain poets, horsemen,
each with his corral and tack,
who ride the watersheds into the alpine
to work for the Parks both sides of the Divide
and for their own delight in
the high meadows, Dall's sheep
along the ridgeline,
are also wordwardens: hunched over keyboards
to conduct the errant words scribbled
on rain-spotted notepaper
into print, to bring to the sterile white pages
the breath-catching lift of a peak's shoulder
treed all the way up to rock,
the scents of a cottonwood grove in July
along the coulee, feel of a worn wood handle
of hoedad or manure fork, of shod hoof on duff,
boot on scree.

          I feel as honored, lucky, blessed
to live amid ranges
as to know these men and their words.
The friendships of men
to me are remotely beautiful
—summits of surpassing grandeur one travels near
and appreciates
and then continues, one's route lightened
by such vistas. Good words, good poems
possess the beauty
of a tree in winter: a formal perfection,
the stalwart bones of a life
rising against a white hillside or field.
But friendship is that tree
leaving out in April, each curled green nub
fulfillment alike of summer
and of shade.

OVERTAKING THE DEAD

If we eat long enough
we catch up to the dead

  —the poet shoveled into a cemetery wall
  with the slogans graffitied around his cubicle
  to honor him
  appearing simplistic compared to
  the awful Fact of death
  Eleven and half years later
  his wife is inserted to join him
  but due to space limitations another woman
  Margarita Valdes
  ends up stacked between them forever

And my phone goes on ringing
apples materializes again on my shopping list
lightbulbs garbage bags
a new block heater for the car

As I age, the dead who have preceded me
—august writers or not—
increasingly seem contemporaries, siblings, equals
Whether they died older or younger than me
I am closer to obtaining their current status
than I am to who I was when we parted
If I believed in certain spells and chants
I would claim we are closer to resuming or initiating a conversation
than to the moment they stopped talking entirely

As I scan books by the dead
I respond more possessively than before:
less *him* or *her*, more *us*
This is what we
—the generation that has vanished, or will soon vanish—

created; not bad, eh?
I trace with a new sense of pride
the lines, the paragraphs
—magnificence attained by a sister
a brother, not some impossibly skilled
or defective
stranger, idol, rival

                    I feel ever-nearer
to these scribblers:
I am certain that by the time I die
I will consider myself entitled to address any of them
by first name
as partners of mine in a profound accomplishment:
to have lived

I tell my students
that the productions of those authors who are personal acquaintances
whose images and obsessions we comprehend
we judge as process:
how the words we have just absorbed
might affect pages they are still fashioning
We weigh each finished piece less harshly
than ones by contemporaries we don't know
whose efforts we assess simply as product:
stanzas, scenes, chapters
viewed stillborn, out of time

I don't mention that now
when I read or reread the dead
I discover I am so purged of envy or scorn
I want to make an encouraging gesture
to pen a note, as I chew on a muffin
Very much enjoyed your latest
I can hardly wait, friend, to see
what you are at work on now

THE DEATH OF AL GRIERSON (1948-2000)

Can of nails, can of nails he hummed
to the wipers' rhythm as his pickup
splashed through the downpour
—he was at work on a song,
steering the back road
rutted and puddled after
weeks of rain. His lights
picked out an earthen cutbank
awash with rivulets, pines at the top,
then along the lane
dense stands of spruce
that dripped shadows and water.
Should it be tin *can of nails?*
Also, who gets the blessed can:
the poor for payment, the nails rusted and bent?
Or are shiny *nails what we mean to give the rich*
as in: 'Work *for your money'?*
Two spots of light brightened and shifted
on the shoulder ahead. He braked hard,
skidding a bit on a muddy patch,
and idled. A deer stared into the headlights,
then with ridiculous dignity
pranced half across the road until
it spooked itself
and bounded for cover, taking the rise on the other side
in three leaps, before disappearing
at a wall of hemlock. *Maybe it's*
cans *of nails,* cans *of nails,* Al half-sung.
I'm so drunk, gunned, blasted,
hammered—happy with his
performance that night: a school classroom
transformed into a cabaret; the kids and parents
laughing and enjoying the music
he had them singing. And in the bar afterwards
people buying him rounds; the organizer of the event

and his bright-eyed girlfriend
offering praise, praise.
Tin cans of nails for you, my friend
no: *my friends*, and the road
began to descend, fenceposts accompanying him—
somebody's field—and at the bottom of the draw
a stream tossing from left to right across the lane,
a river
where one wasn't this afternoon.

He halted and peered as far as his lights.
The road lifted out of the current
twenty feet beyond.
Tin cans, tin cans
of nails, he mused for a moment,
then floored the accelerator. The truck lurched
and the guitar cased beside him
leaning on the passenger seat
tilted toward him so he had to grab the instrument
and set it on the cab floor.
The moment his wheels touched water,
spray rooster-tailed
to block both side windows and
"Wheee," he sang. But the engine
missed once,
twice, sputtered to silence
and he was a sailor. He hit the lights,
cranked the key.
The river hissed and muttered
in the dark. *Tin cans for the poor.*
The truck 15 years old, been through worse,
no doubt, I'll have to get Jamie
give me a tow
in the morning. C'mon, start.
I can't be far
from home, couple miles, what an
adventure. I'll be soaked walking home,
old soak that I am. Nails,

bent nails.

       He saw through the beaded window
a light flicker upstream
—swaying, erratic, as if afloat.
It grew clearer.
Under its oscillating cone
a small flat-bottomed rowboat,
no larger than a cartop, approached,
a poncho-clad figure in the stern
using an oar as
paddle, as pole, as sweep.
The vessel angled
toward him. He thought the craft
would collide with the stalled truck,
but at the last second
the boat in a deft maneuver
swung alongside the vehicle
without a bump. Al rolled down the window, rain
striking the skin of his forehead, his cheeks.

    "Hey,"
he shouted a greeting
over the water's roar. *Hey*, echoed
from under the poncho hood,
the oarsman having seized the lip of
the pickup's front fender.
              Al tried
to see who his rescuer was: neighbor?
Sheriff's deputy? An elderly face
wavered in flowing shadows
as the waters jostled the kerosene lantern
that dangled from a pole lashed to
the forward thwart. *Hill hag
or geezer?* Al chuckled
to himself.

      Step in

—the ancient voice
was unmistakably male.

                      The rain and spray
made Al shiver. *Wouldn't it be best to stay dry*
in the truck, sleep till morning,
sleep it off? If I get a lift to shore
I'll be a drowned rat by the time I'm home,
still have to light the fire,
maybe the storm will have passed
by dawn.

          Step in, the voice repeated,
more insistent.

              What the hell,
Al considered. *This old dude*
has been out risking a dunking
or worse to transport my worthless hide
from the drink, seems sort of churlish
to say, 'No, thanks.' And suppose the flood
worsens, sweeps the damn truck away
with me snoring inside? He cracked the door.
"Whoa, wet out here," he joked,
but the shape holding the craft to the truck
said nothing. "Let me pass you my guitar,"
Al added. The poncho shook its head:
Better where it is. Al reached for his ten-gallon,
stepped gingerly from his metal perch
onto bobbing wood, nearly slipped,
then was abruptly seated
on a drenched thwart amidships, the wet
seeping through the rear of his jeans
so he leaned forward to tuck
his coat beneath him.

              The oarsman
spun with great skill the skiff
upstream from the pickup

and around the rear bumper
and they were pitching downriver
through the storm.
                    "Ride 'em,"
Al shouted, grinning
as he clutched the soaked gunwales to brace himself.
"Thanks for saving me. Name's Al.
I live just up the way." He released one hand
and pointed, but the lane he meant to indicate
was some distance above them now.
"My place is right after Endicott Road. Know it?"
The figure in the stern
seemed focussed on something forward.
Al twisted to gaze ahead,
while the pilot finessed the boat past a wide jam
of stumps, logs, planks.
"What a gale," Al tried again
but the steersman let the rain reply.

                              Tin cans,
tin cans of nails, Al resumed his composition.
Then the river purled into a quieter reach
and his companion announced
You must let your body go.
Al was startled: "Huh?"
You no longer need it. And Al was aware
he was two: the storm had ceased to soak
his jacket through to his shirt and shoulders,
the chill had relinquished his ribs and thighs.
Beside him on the seat,
the body of a person with his features
slumped against him.
It has served its time. Let it go.
The oarsman gestured overboard.
Al felt no heat
from what sagged on him, head dropped.
Suddenly he was filled with pity
intense as revulsion
for this abandoned thing

he had been.
Let it return to water,
the hooded poncho demanded. Al pushed at the puppet,
which toppled into the stream, one arm
lifelessly flailing.
Al watched it sink astern.

      Aren't we going to land?
he inquired, after a minute.

      When we arrive,
the figure said.

    Al stared at the night,
the steady black rain. *Nails, cans of nails.* The river.
Do they sing where we're going? he asked.
There, you are *a song,* the helmsman answered.